Life Levers

Books by Liisa Kyle

You Can Change Your Life: A Workbook to Become the Person You Want to Be

Self-worth Essentials: A Workbook to Understand Yourself, Accept Yourself, Like Yourself, Respect Yourself, Be Confident, Enjoy Yourself, and Love Yourself

Coping in Times of Crisis: Ways to Handle Uncertainty and Navigate the Unknown Future

Overcoming Perfectionism: Solutions for Perfectionists

Get Over It: Overcome Regret, Disappointments, and Past Mistakes

Overcoming Emotional Eating: Coach Yourself to Manage Cravings, Eat Mindfully, and Foster a Healthy Relationship with Food

Making the Most of 2025: A Workbook

Be More Creative: 101 Activities to Unleash and Grow Your Creativity

Making the Most of Your Retirement: Ways to Foster Health, Happiness & Fulfillment at Any Age

Know Yourself Better: Self-Discovery Questions and Activities

Coach Yourself: Self-Coaching Questions and Activities for Self-Discovery and Personal Growth

40 Ways to Enjoy Turning Forty: Make the Most of Your Milestone Birthday to Have the Best Year Ever

50 Ways to Enjoy Turning 50: Make the Most of Your Milestone Birthday to Have the Best Year Ever

Making the Most of Your Milestone Birthday: 52 Ways to Have the Best Year Ever

Coping with the Virus Crisis: Ways to Handle Uncertainty and Navigate the New Normal

You Can Get It Done: Choose What to Do, Plan, Start, Stay on Track, Overcome Obstacles, and Finish

Life Levers

MAKE SMALL CHANGES TO CREATE BIG
IMPROVEMENTS IN YOUR LIFE

Liisa Kyle, PhD

ALEPH BOOK COMPANY
An independent publishing firm
promoted by *Rupa Publications India*

Published in 2018 by Shimmer Press

Published in India in 2025
by Aleph Book Company
7/16 Ansari Road, Daryaganj
New Delhi 110 002

Copyright © Liisa Kyle 2018, 2025

The author has asserted her moral rights.

All rights reserved.

The views and opinions expressed in this book are those of the author and the facts are as reported by her, which have been verified to the extent possible, and the publisher is not in any way liable for the same.

The publisher has used its best endeavours to ensure that URLs for external websites referred to in this book are correct and active at the time of going to press. However, the publisher has no responsibility for the websites and can make no guarantee that a site will remain live or that the content is or will remain appropriate.

No part of this publication may be reproduced, transmitted, or stored in a retrieval system, in any form or by any means, without permission in writing from Aleph Book Company.

For sale in the Indian subcontinent only.

ISBN: 978-93-6523-488-6

1 3 5 7 9 10 8 6 4 2

Printed in India

This book is sold subject to the condition that it shall not, by way of trade or otherwise, be lent, resold, hired out, or otherwise circulated without the publisher's prior consent in any form of binding or cover other than that in which it is published.

Contents

1. The Problem with Change—and the Solution   1
2. What Are Life Levers?   13
3. Implementing Life Levers   21
4. Gratitude is a Highly Effective Life Lever   29
5. Forgiveness is a Highly Effective Life Lever   46
6. Mindfulness is a Highly Effective Life Lever   57
7. Using Life Levers to Solve a Problem   75
8. Using Life Levers to Accomplish Something   88
9. Using Life Levers to Improve Your Life   106
10. What Works Best for You?   115

Acknowledgements   119

CHAPTER 1

The Problem with Change—and the Solution

Change is possible.

People *can* change. For the past twenty years, as a life coach and management consultant, I've helped people make real, purposeful changes using proven techniques and processes. It's actually quite straightforward.

To change, you need:

- a clear vision of what you want to do
- a willingness to change that exceeds any inherent resistance, and
- specific, doable action steps

It's a straightforward process…but it isn't easy. Change is challenging. If real change were easy, everyone would be living their ideal life.

WHY IS CHANGE SO DIFFICULT?

When people, groups, or organizations fail to change, it's because of one or more of the following reasons:

1. There isn't a sufficiently clear or compelling vision of the desired outcome.

It's hard to move in the desired direction when you don't know or don't care or don't like where you're aiming. Your efforts can be shooting off in competing directions, essentially cancelling out any potential progress on any given track.

2. There is an inadequate awareness of what the problem actually is—let alone the variables influencing it.

We've all seen great companies fall off the rails by chasing phantom demons instead of addressing their true corporate flaws. Most of my coaching clients come to me for help with a specific concern, unaware that the true issue requiring resolution is something else entirely.

3. It's not clear what, exactly, you're supposed to do to change.

To change, we need to identify specific, doable actions. If these are too vague or overly ambitious, they won't get us very far. If you want to "be happy" but don't know where or how to start, you won't experience much progress.

4. The natural initial response to any change—even a positive change—is fear.

This is a biological fact of the human experience: Anything new is perceived as a threat until proven otherwise. Until that initial fear is addressed and dealt with, our clever minds intervene to protect us.

5. Our clever minds are really good at protecting us.

Our brains protect us by camouflaging the true issues and by actively resisting change. Resistance can be disguised as procrastination or confusion or laziness or distractedness or thirty other things. This is often fueled by inner doubts that we really can make the change.

The internal sources of resistance can be so strong, they are difficult to overcome. If there is insufficient will to overcome the resistance, change won't happen.

6. External factors may hamper our progress.

External priorities may compete for our attention and energy, interfering with our efforts. Ever notice how when you decide to make a change in one part of your life, other parts go haywire? You resolve to improve your fitness…and as soon as you join the gym, suddenly your workload doubles and your kids need chauffeuring and your keys keep disappearing and your cat gets sick and company descends on your household and your fridge starts making strange sounds. Before you know it, poof! A month has passed since you've worked out.

7. External sources of resistance can also take their toll.

Think of a time when you embarked on a course of change and then you encountered parental disapproval or a friend's indifference or an acquaintance's jealousy or a reviewer's ire or something else that quashed your resolve or enthusiasm. To make a change, the strength of your will must be greater than the total of all external resistance you encounter.

◆

These are the main seven reasons changes fail. Their effects magnify each other: *The bigger the proposed change, the more fear, the more resistance, the harder to implement, and the more challenging it is.*

Despite all this, change *is* possible. If there is something you *really* want to change, you can. The traditional approach is to implement a strategic change plan, featuring a clear vision and specific, doable action steps, including ways to overcome any resistance.

However, for many people, it's not possible or practical to successfully implement a full strategic change plan—especially if you are trying to do this all by yourself, with little support or guidance, and with everything else you've got going on.

SO, WHAT'S THE SOLUTION?

It's great if you can devise and implement a full strategic change plan. But it's not the only option. Rather than trying to implement a big change plan, an alternative is to go small: What is the tiniest possible, easiest change you can make in your life right now? What one tiny adjustment can you make right now, today, given your unique personal preferences and circumstances?

For some of you, this is all that's needed: a prompt to make small shifts in your life and to watch what happens.

Most of you, however, will require more convincing. I've written this book for you.

As a PhD working on four continents over the past two decades, I've seen people, groups, and organizations make massive improvements by starting small. Tiny shifts in thought, word, or deed, consistently applied, can be leveraged into enormous changes.

If you doubt the value of this approach, please pause and contemplate how small adjustments can lead to huge improvements.

Consider how tiny actions, applied consistently, can establish a healthy or helpful new habit. Sandy began walking around the block each day, every day. She can't really remember why she started but once she did, she liked it. It felt good to be outside. She enjoyed looking at people's gardens and pets and saying "Hi" to her neighbors. After each jaunt around the block, she returned feeling a little refreshed.

Gradually, Sandy extended her walks. She explored other

streets around her home. She found a sports path near the water that was very pleasant to walk along. A friend invited her to try a gentle hike nearby. She enjoyed it. She started looking for other such outings.

Within a matter of months, Sandy joined a local walking club. By the end of the year, she was fitter than she'd been in years. Along the way, she'd met new friends and enriched her social life.

Note that Sandy didn't PLAN to get fit or to make new friends—she made a tiny change in behavior that, over time, had big impacts on her health and social life.

Small actions can also be used to accomplish specific goals: Large, unwieldy projects can be completed by breaking them down into tiny, doable pieces. Mark enjoyed blogging and wanted to write a book. But every time he sat down to start, his hands would freeze above the keyboard.

He consulted a friend who was a writer. "A whole book! How am I going to write an entire book?"

"Okay, so you're freaked out by writing a whole book. How do you feel about writing one page?"

"A page? A page is nothing. I could write a page right now."

"So do it. Just write one page."

Mark tried it. He sat at his computer and wrote. The task of aiming for one page was much less daunting than the notion of creating an entire book.

He texted his writer friend: "I did it! I wrote the page. Now what?"

"Do it again. Rinse and repeat. Every time you sit down to write, just aim for one page."

"That's it?"

"That's it. Each page you write is progress. If you can keep at it consistently, you'll finish your book."

Mark committed to try this new approach. He figured that he could reasonably aim to write a page a day, at least three days a week. Each writing session was fun and gratifying. Each completed page was a little victory. Every week, Mark could witness the pages adding up, bit by bit. The more he wrote, the more he was motivated to write. Sometimes he was able to find an extra hour on the weekend to "sneak in" some extra writing.

By implementing this tiny change in behavior (writing one page per day)—and sticking with it—Mark completed writing the first draft of his book in ten months.

There is no limit to what can be accomplished by small changes in behavior. Perhaps even bigger impacts, however, come from tiny shifts in **thought**. As Daniel Webster said, "Mind is the great lever of all things; human thought is the process by which human ends are ultimately answered."

Consider the thought "I have to go to work." This sentiment conveys an obligation that can taint your professional efforts with dread and pessimism. It can weigh you down and impair your professional relationships. Your personal relationships can take a hit, too, because odds are high that you're not a pleasant person to be with after a day of "*having* to work".

What if, when you stop and think about it, you're actually grateful to have a job, to provide whatever service or duty someone is paying you do to, to be earning income when many people are unemployed. Maybe you'd much rather have something of worth do to—rather than sitting at home, broke, and unfulfilled.

If so, then consider what happens by shifting your thought from "I *have* to go to work" to "I *get* to go to work." Imagine how this tiny change in thought can generate completely different results: When you believe you "get" to go to work, you are happier to be there, doing whatever you are doing, interacting with whomever you encounter. You are more pleasant to be with at work and at home.

This one tiny adjustment in thought can generate massive improvements in many areas of your life.

It's also an example of how a tiny shift in the words we use can have big consequences. It's the difference between calling something a "problem" or a "challenge"...or an "opportunity". It's the difference between saying you "will try to do" something versus saying you "will do" it.

Among the words we use, perhaps the most powerful are those we apply to ourselves. Consider the words you use to describe yourself—or that other people have labeled you. These words shape how we think about ourselves. For example, I distinctly recall the afternoon when one elementary school chum expressed her exasperation that I "start all these different projects and never finish any of them! You're such a flake!" The label stung and, apparently, it stuck.

It wasn't until years later, I realized (to my surprise and horror) that I had internalized the "flake" label. Somehow, deep down, I had been harboring the notion that I was an irresponsible dilettante dabbling in random things for no good reason. As soon as I recognized this hidden belief, I also saw it was untrue. As a child, my week was crammed with all sorts of lessons, activities, and hobbies. Sure, some projects didn't get finished but many did. Actually, I was a responsible, conscientious, punctual person who was interested and involved in a lot of different activities. It's still true today. I'm interested in many things.

Thinking of myself as "interested in many things" rather than as a "flake" is a small change in wording that has had a huge impact on me. Whereas "flake" caused me to feel shame and guilt, "interested in many things" validates my different activities and projects. It encourages me to learn and grow and pursue new directions. I feel gratified by my multiple pursuits, rather than ashamed. "Yes, I'm interested in many things!" I'll shout it proudly. Those words feel so much better.

This brings us to the next point. Consider what happens when you experience a tiny shift in feeling. Remember the moment you fell in love with someone? Or maybe you weren't too crazy about a particular person, and then something shifted so you viewed them more positively or compassionately. (*Gosh! I thought Alex was pretty grumpy but I had no idea his kid was battling cancer. Under the circumstances, he's positively sunny!*)

Have you experienced that moment of relief of truly forgiving someone—or being forgiven? Either involves a shift in feeling that cements or improves the relationship.

Or perhaps you've been lied to by someone you considered to be a friend—creating a shift in feeling that damaged or ended the relationship.

This next activity is an opportunity for you to examine how tiny changes have led to big improvements in your life. To get the most out of this activity, write out your answers. By doing so, you will elicit deeper insights and generate more ideas.

ACTIVITY

1. Think of a **tiny change in behavior** that led to improvements in your life. *This might have been a change in routine or the establishment of a new habit or the development of a new technique or skill.*

    - Describe what occurred. What was the change?

- What were the consequences?

- What was the experience like for you?

- How challenging was it?

- How rewarding was it?

2. Think of a **tiny change in thought** that had a big impact. *This might have been a change in opinion or belief or attitude about someone or something. It might have been a small change in expectation or perspective or understanding.*

    - Describe what occurred. What was the change?

    - What were the consequences?

    - What was the experience like for you?

    - How challenging was it?

- How rewarding was it?

3. Think of a **tiny change in words** that had a big impact. *This might have been a change in the words you use to describe yourself or someone else. It might have been a reframing of an activity, place, or experience.*

    - Describe what occurred. What was the change?

    - What were the consequences?

    - What was the experience like for you?

    - How challenging?

    - How rewarding?

4. Think of a **tiny change in feeling** that had big consequences. *This might have been a change of heart, a reduction in fear, forgiving someone or being forgiven, falling in love, or losing trust in someone.*

    - Describe what occurred. What was the change?

- What were the consequences?

- What was the experience like for you?

- How challenging?

- How rewarding?

LIFE LEVERS

When tiny changes can yield big results, you are getting more leverage out of your efforts. The experience tends to be easy, rather than challenging.

That's the beauty of "Life Levers"—we can do less to gain more. We can make small, easy adjustments that can eventually lead to big improvements in our lives.

The purpose of this book is to help you identify and apply Life Levers that will work for *you*. What tiny adjustments can you make that will create big improvements in your life, given your unique circumstances and preferences?

HOW TO GET THE MOST OUT OF THIS BOOK

Begin by reading the next chapter to understand more about how levers work.

Then use Chapter Three to implement the Life Lever approach in your own life.

The remainder of the book is a reference guide for you to consult as needed. You can read it in any order. You can skip whatever chapters aren't of interest right now. By design there is a lot of overlap and repetition so that you can utilize any chapter as a stand-alone guide.

If you'd like to learn more about specific, highly effective levers:

- Chapter 4 describes how to use Gratitude as a Life Lever.
- Chapter 5 examines the power of Forgiveness as a Life Lever.
- Chapter 6 explores how you can use Mindfulness as a Life Lever.

If you have a problem to solve, turn to Chapter 7.

If you'd like to accomplish something, turn to Chapter 8.

If you're not sure what you want but something seems "off" and you'd like to change it, turn to Chapter 9.

This book is designed to be written on so mark it up! Make it yours.

It's up to you to determine how much you'd like to get out of the experience of working through this book. The more you put into the activities, the more you'll get out.

CHAPTER 2

What Are Life Levers?

A lever is a device that magnifies force.

Imagine a boulder so heavy you can't budge it. With the right tool—maybe a long, strong crowbar—it's possible that you can use a relatively small effort to move that boulder.

© Lisa Rothstein, www.LisaRothstein.com

If we apply this concept to your life, the "boulder" might be a problem you're trying to solve or a goal you're trying to accomplish. Or maybe it's just the weight of the world: something doesn't feel "right" or "good" and you don't quite know what's wrong.

A Life Lever is a change in thought, word, feeling, or deed that shifts your "boulder".

With the right Life Lever, you can exert a tiny effort—i.e., make a small shift in thought, word, feeling, or deed—to create big improvements in your life. By consistently applying the lever that works for you, you can solve problems, establish healthy habits, get things done, improve your relationships, and more.

Archimedes said, "Give me a lever long enough…and I shall move the world."

I say, "With the right lever, you can change your life."

The trick is to start small. To find a tiny adjustment that can start to move things in a new direction. Consider this diagram:

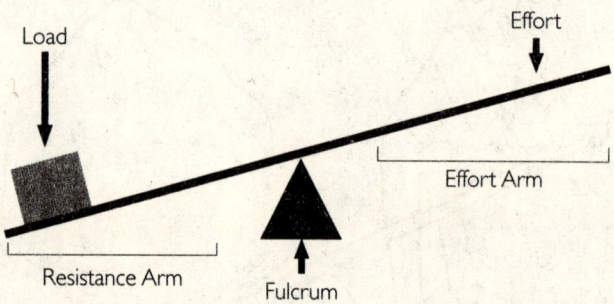

Image via commons.wikimedia.org

Think of the Load as your "boulder". It's the reason you're reading this book. It could be something you'd like to do or a problem you're trying to solve or some other burden you're bearing.

The Fulcrum represents your current situation.

Resistance is everything that's keeping you in your current

position. This includes internal resistance (such as fear, confusion, procrastination, guilt, laziness, distractedness, or perfectionism) as well as external factors such as competing priorities, competition, and the influence of others (disapproval/jealousy/indifference/criticism, etc.).

Effort is what you have to do to shift the load.

As soon as you shift the load even the tiniest bit, you've achieved The Tipping Point—the point at which you have overcome resistance and started a real change.

♦

THE LIFE LEVER APPROACH

Make a tiny change to create big improvements in your life. You can use it to get things done, to solve challenges, to disrupt unhealthy habits, and more.

© Lisa Rothstein, www.LisaRothstein.com

STEP ONE: CHOOSE A TINY CHANGE AS YOUR LEVER

What is the smallest change that can shift the load? What's the tiniest effort you can make to get your "boulder" to start to move?

This could be a tiny change in behavior…or it might be even smaller. It could be a shift in thought or a change in feeling or even a modification of the words you use.

The idea here is to find some small adjustment in your life to start your boulder moving.

STEP TWO: START

Begin. Apply your tiny change and see what happens.

Once your boulder moves even a smidge, you've overcome resistance and disrupted inertia. Yay! You've reached the Tipping Point. Once things start moving, it's so much easier to keep them rolling.

It's basic physics. The first part of Newton's First Law of Motion says, "A body at rest will remain at rest unless an outside force acts on it." A body at rest stays at rest until it gets a nudge. You've seen this in your own life. It can be challenging indeed to start something…but once you do, it's easier to keep going.

STEP THREE: CARRY ON. MONITOR AND ADJUST ACCORDINGLY

Once your situation begins to shift, do what makes sense, given your unique circumstances and preferences.

As things proceed, keep track. Ask yourself this question every few days: To what extent are things moving in a better direction?

Do what works for you. If the initial change in thought, word, feeling, or deed is moving things in a better direction, carry on.

The more consistent you are, the more progress you will experience.

Once you're accustomed to a particular change, you can push the lever a little more to get a bigger effect. For example, once walking five minutes a day becomes a part of your regular routine, you may wish to aim for ten.

However, if you're not seeing progress, what adjustments need to be made? Do you need to do more or less with your chosen lever? Is it time to try a different lever?

If something starts going in an unhelpful direction, make the needed adjustments. Cease doing what isn't helpful and try something else. Again, less is more. If you make tiny changes, it's easier to correct your course as needed.

◆

MORE ABOUT LIFE LEVERS

1. You don't have to know what your "boulder" is.

The Life Lever approach works when you are seeking to solve a particular problem or start a healthy habit or make progress towards a goal. And it *also* works when you don't really know what you want. Maybe you just feel "off" or "blah" or unfulfilled. No problem. Just make one tiny shift in thought, word, feeling, or deed and watch what happens. If you sense positive results, carry on. Monitor and adjust accordingly. If things seem the same, try a different lever.

2. There are infinite possible levers.

No need to get caught up seeking the "perfect" lever. *Anything* that starts to shift your burden is just fine. No need to procrastinate or fret or deliberate—just pick something—anything—and monitor what happens.

3. The process should be easy and comfortable (i.e., free of fear).

The reason Life Levers work is that they create changes so small they don't elicit our natural fear response. If the change is so tiny it doesn't frighten us, we don't trigger our natural protective mechanisms (such as procrastination or confusion or distraction or laziness or any of the thirty other ways our clever minds resist change).

If you find yourself resisting the Lever you've chosen, it may be that you're trying to do too much. Make it smaller. Make it laughably tiny. Make it easy and comfortable.

4. Make it easy to monitor your progress.

The simpler the better. It might be a matter of asking yourself once every few days, "How am I doing?"

Is follow-through a challenge for you? Are you someone who starts things with great zeal, only to find yourself, a month later, wondering, "Now what was it I wanted to be doing? And why haven't I?" If this sounds like you, consider making a weekly appointment with yourself to assess your progress. Book five minutes on your schedule each week to check your progress to pause, assess how you're doing, and decide how best to proceed.

If you are implementing a change in behavior, sometimes it's helpful to make a visual representation so you can see the overall pattern. For example, comedian Jerry Seinfeld writes a joke a day, no exceptions. He marks his calendar with a big "X" after he completes his daily task, with the intention of never breaking the chain of X's.

Might something similar work for you? For example, if you are aiming to walk ten minutes a day, you could give yourself a star on your calendar for every day you do. At the end of the week, if you see lots of stars on your calendar, it's gratifying. Or if your calendar page is empty, you can decide what adjustments you need to make. Perhaps ten minutes a day is too much for you right now. Maybe you need to aim for five instead.

If you want to do something you can quantify numerically—such as losing weight or writing a particular number of pages or spending a certain amount of time on a project—you can create a visual representation of your progress by graphing the relevant numbers.

For example, when Maria wanted to trim down, she weighed herself every day and plotted the numbers on a graph. Weight tends to fluctuate up and down under the best of circumstances and, when you're dieting, it's easy to get caught up in particular numbers (and to despair when they go in the "wrong" direction). The graph Maria made was very helpful because she could see that, despite many minor upticks, there was a clear downward trend in her weight, overall. She could see the line going in the desired direction (downward-ish), which motivated her to keep doing what she was doing.

5. It's okay to swap levers, going forward.

Often, someone will use one lever to get the ball rolling…and then change to other levers at different times, as things unfold. It's more important to experiment and find what will work for you, given your unique circumstances and preferences.

The idea here is to aim for consistent progress. It really doesn't matter which levers you use to keep things moving—so long as they continue in your desired direction.

6. Aim for progress, not perfection.

Job One is to get things moving. Once you've achieved the Tipping Point, your mission is to keep going in a positive direction. You're not trying to do things to some particular standard, let alone "perfectly". Aim for incremental improvements over time. Is this better than it was a week ago? A month ago? If yes, great. If no, what adjustments are needed?

7. It's all about you.

This approach is meant to be personalized and tailored to suit you. You know everything you've got going on in your life. You know what works well for you and what doesn't. You know what motivates you and what squelches your enthusiasm. Use what you know about yourself, your preferences, and your circumstances to make changes you can sustain.

If in doubt, ask yourself: What has worked well for me in the past? Could it work now or would I need to modify things somehow?

♦

Ready to try the Life Lever approach? Please turn to the next chapter.

CHAPTER 3

Implementing Life Levers

The purpose of this chapter is to guide you through the Life Lever Approach, step by step. Pick a Lever—any Lever—then actually apply it in your own life. For best results, actually write out your answers to the questions in this chapter.

STEP ONE: CHOOSE A TINY CHANGE AS YOUR LEVER

Clear five minutes for private reflection. Reflect on your current life.

> What tiny changes could you make that might improve things for you? Make a list. Consider shifts in thought, word, feeling, or deed. Jot down whatever pops into your head.
>
> Review your list and pick something—anything—as your Lever. Circle it. Proceed to Step Two.

TROUBLESHOOTING

If you had difficulty making a list of possible changes, answer the following questions:

What tiny changes could you make in your **behavior** that might improve things for you? Consider actions, habits, and routines. Think about things you are doing that you might do less of—or more of. Are there things you are not doing at the moment that would be helpful?

What tiny changes could you make in your **thinking** that might improve things for you? Your list might include a change in opinion, or belief, or attitude about someone or something. It could include a change in expectation, or perspective, or understanding.

Now review your lists and pick something—anything—as your Lever. Proceed to Step Two.

TROUBLESHOOTING

If you still drew a blank, consider a task or goal you are seeking to accomplish.

Is there something you want to do or get done? (*E.g., lose five pounds, improve a relationship, reduce or quit an unhelpful habit, travel somewhere you've wanted to go, organize your closets, learn to play piano, improve your level of fitness, write a book, increase your income.*)

> Pick one specific goal or task: _____
>
> What tiny changes could you make in thought, word, feeling, or deed that would move you a wee bit closer to your goal? Make a list.
>
>
>
>
>
> Review your list and pick something—anything—as your Lever. Circle it. Proceed to Step Two.

♦

STEP TWO: START

Beginning right now, implement the tiny change you chose in Step One.

That's all there is to it. Just do it.

Proceed to Step Three.

> ### TROUBLESHOOTING
>
> If you find yourself hesitating to get started, answer this:
> Is your "tiny change" too big?
> If so, how can you make it small enough to actually do it?

Make the necessary adjustments and start.
If the size of the change feels doable but you still need a nudge to start, ask yourself the following:

- What might I gain by starting? Make a list.

- What might I lose or miss by not starting? Make a list.

- What reward can I give myself for starting? List fitting, easy treats.

Then start. And when you do, be sure to give yourself a treat. At a minimum, check in once a week.

STEP THREE: CARRY ON. MONITOR AND ADJUST ACCORDINGLY

Once you've begun, it's just a matter of continuing. Do what you intend. For example, if your plan is to walk ten minutes a day, do so.

Keep track of your progress in the simplest, easiest way you can. For example, you could put stars, checkmarks, or emojis on your calendar for every day you do what you intend.

Then check in every few days to analyze how you're doing.

MONITOR YOUR PROGRESS

A. Keep Track

- What are simple, easy ways you can track your progress?

B. Analyze and Adjust

Every few days (or once a week) ask yourself:

- To what extent am I doing what I intended?
- What differences do I notice?
- What adjustments need to be made, if any? At a minimum, check in once a week.

Seek small, consistent shifts in your desired direction. Be kind to yourself. Praise any forward momentum. Your goal is to aim for progress, rather than perfection.

After a few weeks, see what consequences you notice.

C. Progress Check

Schedule an appointment with yourself for a month from now. On that date, pause to answer the following:

- Overall, how are you doing, compared with how you were when you started?

- What differences do you notice?

- Going forward, what adjustments are needed, if any?

D. Adjust Accordingly

- If you are experiencing progress, carry on. Make adjustments when and if they are necessary.
- For example, when it seems like you should do more or less, do so.
- If it's time to switch Levers, do so.

TROUBLESHOOTING

If you notice, "Gosh, it's been months since I thought about my progress," pause and take stock.

Maybe you're already "there". Perhaps you've already achieved what you wanted or gotten sufficient benefit out of the process. If so, great. Reward yourself for what you've accomplished.

If, instead, you have not been progressing, ask:
- Are you still applying your chosen Lever?

If so, what adjustments are needed?

If not, ask, why not?

If it wasn't working for you, pick another Lever.

If it was working for you but you got distracted or otherwise occupied, simply resume.

TROUBLESHOOTING

If you resume, then find yourself off track again before too long, ask why:

- Are you being sidetracked by distractions? If so, how could you reduce or remove them?

- Do you need to schedule specific times or places to focus on this Lever?

- Would a particular time of day work better for you?

- Do you need a tinier Lever?

- Do you need a different Lever?

- Is there a Lever that would be easier or more comfortable for you to apply at this time?

Once you've had the experience of purposefully making a tiny change that led to big improvements, you have witnessed the strength of the Life Levers approach. It's much easier to make a small change than to implement a full strategic change plan.

THREE HIGHLY EFFECTIVE LIFE LEVERS

Any tiny change in thought, word, feeling, or deed can be a Life Lever…and yet certain Levers are special. There are three in particular that are unusually powerful and highly effective in solving problems, getting things done, improving relationships, and more.

These Levers aren't complicated. In fact, they are so simple and easy that some people dismiss them because they seem "too easy".

In my two decades of helping people make real change in their life, I've seen extraordinary progress when people use Gratitude, Forgiveness, and/or Mindfulness as Life Levers.

They are simple. They are easy. I encourage you to try them.

We'll examine each of them in turn.

CHAPTER 4

Gratitude is a Highly Effective Life Lever

© *Lisa Rothstein, www.LisaRothstein.com*

One of the most powerful, effective Life Levers is Gratitude. It's also one of the easiest to use. All you have to do is express your sincere thanks.

Some people dismiss Gratitude as being little more than a polite convention. (*Sure, I say "please" and "thank you". So what?*) Holders of this perspective are missing out on the many, many benefits of Gratitude when applied sincerely and purposefully.

◆

WHAT CAN GRATITUDE DO?

Whenever you are truly thankful, you have the opportunity to:

- highlight what's working well in your life
- feel better about your current circumstances and experiences
- honor your past experiences and accomplishments
- foster more of what you enjoy
- elevate your mood
- dispel dissatisfaction
- solve problems
- detect "blessings in disguise"
- improve your relationships
- combat perfectionism and judgment
- counteract pessimism and negativity

◆

GRATITUDE BASICS

Gratitude is the expression of sincere appreciation or thanks. It can be a matter of thinking a truly grateful thought. It can be done silently, privately, and internally. It can be spoken out loud, or written on paper, or typed in digital format. It can be uttered publicly or shared electronically. It doesn't really matter how, or where, or in what format your Gratitude is expressed.

There is, however, a catch. You have to mean it. Your Gratitude must be sincere for the Lever to shift things in your life.

Consider your own experiences. Think of a time in which someone had to be prompted to thank you. Or when you complimented someone without really meaning it. It is unlikely that either incident felt very good.

Now compare this with true appreciation: Maybe you took a moment to savor something. Perhaps you gave someone a sincere compliment. Possibly an event made you realize you'd been taking something or someone for granted—and ushered in a new wave of appreciation. True Gratitude feels good. Hence the word "gratifying". Sincere Gratitude improves things—our mood, our relationships, our perspectives, and more.

Some people have difficulty expressing Gratitude when they are in situations where they are so overwhelmed or hopeless or stressed that they feel like they have nothing to be thankful for.

If that sounds like you, consider this: wherever you are, whatever your situation, you have things you can appreciate. You have air to breathe and the respiratory system to do so. You have the capacity to read and to think. You have the opportunity to experience different activities, places, and situations. You can appreciate the highlights of your life so far. You can be grateful for this very moment.

◆

GRATITUDE 2.0

Have you tried a daily Gratitude practice? Many people try making a daily list of things for which they are thankful.

Often, this feels good for the first few iterations…then gets to be a rote exercise. (*Yeah yeah yeah. I'm grateful for my relationships, my home, my car, my lunch, the weather, yada yada yada.*)

When Gratitude is devoid of true sentiment, it loses its power as a Life Lever.

Fortunately, this is easy to fix. A daily Gratitude practice can be made very powerful indeed with one small amendment: Rather than just listing things for which you are grateful, express

why. This technique worked for Einstein and it will work for you.

This small alteration—the additional explanation of **why** you're grateful—elevates and deepens the sincerity of your gratitude. Rather than jotting down "my home office" and racing onto the next item on your Gratitude list, it's much more powerful to specify your rationale.

I'm grateful for my home office because it's comfortable, and well organized, and pleasingly decorated and is full of books I adore, plus it provides a pleasant, quiet space to accomplish my work efficiently and effectively.

I call this enhanced daily practice "Gratitude 2.0". It's a simple, quick, powerful activity that can shift many areas of your life with minimal effort. Do yourself a favor. Try it right now.

ACTIVITY

Write down five things for which you are thankful and explain why.

1.

2.

3.

4.

5.

BONUS ACTIVITY: Read your answers out loud.

Notice the difference from simply listing your blessings? If you'd like to supercharge the impact of your Gratitude, make a daily practice of listing things you truly appreciate—and why. Bonus points if you read your list aloud.

How was the experience for you? Most people find it pleasant and satisfying.

GRATITUDE 2.0

STEP ONE:
Clear some uninterrupted time for private reflection. Have ready a pen and paper or your computer or tablet.

STEP TWO:

Jot down at least five things for which you are grateful. As you list each item you appreciate, state why.

"I'm grateful for X because…"
"I'm thankful for Y because…"

STEP THREE (OPTIONAL):

Re-read your list. As you read, aim to actually feel a sense of Gratitude.
    This isn't strictly necessary but if you choose to re-read your list, you boost the potency of this practice.
    It's even more powerful if you read your list aloud. You can do this alone or with someone else. My coaching clients find it especially effective to share their lists with a Gratitude Partner—a trusted person they contact for a quick phone call during which each person reads their Gratitude list.

STEP FOUR:

Repeat the preceding steps several more times this week, each time choosing (at least) five *new* things to appreciate.

Note: The Gratitude 2.0 Practice can be adapted to suit your unique preferences and circumstances. If five Gratitude items per session seems like too few, aim for seven or ten. If five seems like too many, aim for three. Given your schedule, how many days a week can you reasonably commit to do the practice? Every day? Five days a week? Every other day? Twice a week? Once a week?

The exact numbers don't matter. What's important is to create a pattern that you do consistently.

The Gratitude 2.0 Practice is an easy way to acknowledge and reinforce things that are working well in your life.

I'm thankful my dogs need to be exercised daily, so that I get to go for a walk every day—to move my desk-bound carcass to spend time outside, in nature, enjoying my neighborhood while keeping my dogs healthy and happy.

The more you express Gratitude for the people, things, and activities you enjoy, the more you will experience—and the better you will feel about your current circumstances and experiences.

You can apply this practice to EVERY area of your life. You can be grateful for aspects of

- your physical body and health
- your living situation
- your relationships
- your experiences
- your work and career
- your activities, progress, and successes
- your resources and material possessions
- your mind, ideas, and thinking
- nice surprises
- your learning, growth, and personal development
- your leisure activities
- your pets
- technology
- resolution of problems or dilemmas
- your goals and dreams
- your personal strengths
- your mind

- nature
- the air you breathe
- access to clean water
- services you receive
- your neighbors and community
- your planet, solar system, galaxy, and universe
- your existence

Gratitude 2.0 is a great way to acknowledge the highlights of your life so far. In addition to generating Gratitude items from your current life, consider features of your past for which you are thankful. These might include aspects of

- your childhood
- your family
- your friends
- your mentors, guides, and teachers
- your past relationships (personal and professional)
- kindnesses you have received
- love you have experienced
- your education
- life lessons you have learned
- your personal growth and development
- your life milestones
- your turning points
- your personal accomplishments
- moments of peace and tranquillity you have experienced
- historical events which have benefitted you
- role models who have inspired you

To the extent you make Gratitude 2.0 a regular practice, you are apt to find your mood lifting. It's one of the most effective ways to dispel dissatisfaction or the blues or the blahs.

When you really get into it, Gratitude 2.0 seems to fuel itself. The more you do it, the more appreciation you are apt to find seeping into your day. Even a mundane observation can trigger a brief burst of thankfulness. (*"I'm grateful for this alarm clock because I can sleep soundly knowing that I won't be late in the morning."*)

◆

ON A PERSONAL NOTE

I have witnessed the power of the Gratitude 2.0 Practice first hand. I've seen miracles unfold in my own life as well as the lives of my coaching clients, friends, and family.

If the only thing you take from this book is the Gratitude 2.0 Practice, I'd be thrilled because I know that if you are consistent in expressing sincere Gratitude on a regular basis, you will improve your life. You don't need a grand plan or a vision if you have Gratitude. By consistently expressing thankfulness for the things that you truly appreciate, you will experience more of them.

◆

OTHER WAYS TO USE GRATITUDE AS A LIFE LEVER

The powerful Gratitude 2.0 Practice is one way to wield Gratitude as a Life Lever. You can also apply Gratitude in other ways for specific purposes. Gratitude is a terrific Lever to:

- counteract pessimism and/or negativity
- detect "blessings in disguise"
- improve relationships
- counter perfectionism and judgment

USING GRATITUDE TO COUNTERACT PESSIMISM OR NEGATIVITY

If you find yourself feeling negative or pessimistic about someone or something, you can instantly improve the situation by applying sincere Gratitude.

It's also a way to re-frame things that aren't going so well into a different, more palatable perspective. If a day is challenging, it's helpful to pause and think about what *is* working well.

> *Okay, so this project has hit another roadblock; however, I'm grateful I have a job and an income because I help support my family. I'm so thankful I have this project because it shows that my boss believes I'm up to the challenge, and because I'd rather be working on something difficult than be bored and underutilized. It's been a stressful day so far, but I'm grateful that my workday is concluding and I can go home because the remainder of my day will be easier and more pleasant.*

When we go through difficult experiences, it's helpful to mine the experience for whatever good might have come out of it.

Frieda was involved in a car accident. She used Gratitude to put her experience in perspective:

> *I'm thankful no one was seriously injured.*
>
> *I'm grateful the responsible person's insurance is paying for the damage.*
>
> *I'm thankful for this reminder to be more vigilant of other vehicles around me and to keep a larger cushion of space around me when I'm driving because I will be safer.*
>
> *I'm so grateful for the opportunity to cease taking my car for granted because really, it's a privilege and a luxury to own a vehicle and to be able to go wherever I want, whenever I*

want. It makes my life much easier, and I can organize my activities much more efficiently than if I had to rely on public transportation.

Shawn was laid up with a health challenge for a prolonged period. He used Gratitude to come to terms with the situation:

I'm thankful for this opportunity to slow down and heal my body because I am countering my tendency to rush around in a stressed state.

I'm grateful for this health challenge because through the help, assistance, and support I've received, I see who really cares about me—and who does not.

I'm grateful for all the music I've listened to during my convalescence because I've enjoyed it, and it's made the time more pleasant.

I'm thankful for this period of immobility because I've been inspired to call friends and relatives who live elsewhere, and I've enjoyed catching up with them.

I'm thankful for this period of downtime during my convalescence because it's provided opportunities for personal reflection, for thinking about my life, and for re-examining my priorities.

I'm grateful for this reminder to stop taking my health for granted and to take good care of my body because it's shown me that my health needs to be a higher priority, going forward.

ACTIVITY

Pick something in your life about which you feel negatively. List as many positives as you can about the situation.

It can be challenging to detect opportunities for Gratitude when facing a problem, but to the extent you do, you can put things in perspective. You can remind yourself that this challenge is only one part of your current life. You may discern some solutions or ways to improve the situation or make the best of it. You might detect some "blessings in disguise".

USING GRATITUDE TO DETECT BLESSINGS IN DISGUISE

Whenever you go through something challenging, you have the opportunity to use Gratitude to recognize Blessings in Disguise.

Consider Debra's experience. Her young daughter was repeatedly admitted to the hospital with life-threatening asthma. The medical bills were enormous—far beyond her family's means. As a result of the financial toll, they were evicted from the house they loved. It felt like rock bottom. Moving day was humiliating, physically demanding, and just darn gross. As they started shifting furniture, they found mold behind the couch, behind the dressers, and in the closets. They had to throw out furniture, clothes, towels, and linens.

About a year after they moved, Debra realized that her daughter hadn't been sick in many months. She deduced that the mold in their previous abode had been exacerbating her daughter's asthma. Being evicted seemed like rock bottom but really it was a Blessing in Disguise. Once they were living somewhere else, her daughter was much healthier and the medical bills ceased. The move may have even saved her daughter's life.

Louisa is another case in point. She underwent simple day surgery and things went horribly wrong. She went into anaphylactic shock and almost died. Doesn't sound like much of a gift or blessing, does it? But when Louisa applied Gratitude, she found plenty.

"Well, this experience certainly did wake me up," she wrote to me recently. "I am no longer complacent or bored. I am grateful for the people in my life and mindful of how I treat people. Normally we keep birthdays pretty quiet but I decided then and there that I was never taking another birthday for granted. We had forty people here to help me celebrate my fiftieth birthday. I joined the gym and am getting very active. I'm enjoying life and renewing old friendships and nurturing the existing ones. I just joined a yoga class and am going to sign up for conversational Italian so I can be fluent enough for a future trip to Italy."

> ### ACTIVITY
>
> Think of a "Blessing in Disguise" in your own life—some challenge or apparent setback that ended up yielding unexpected benefits.
>
> Describe what happened.
>
> What blessings emerged, eventually?

USING GRATITUDE TO IMPROVE RELATIONSHIPS

If you want to feel closer to someone, use Gratitude as a Lever. Write out ten things you appreciate about them—and why.

Bonus points if you share your list with the person—but you needn't do so to experience the positive effects of expressing Gratitude. Somehow, even when you do this privately, it seems to shift the energy in the relationship. When you are clearer about what you appreciate about this person, it warms and deepens your interactions.

Or, in the case of people who are no longer in your life or are no longer alive, Gratitude can enhance your memory of the relationship. It can dissolve whatever residual resentments remain.

Gratitude is particularly useful when you have (or had) a complicated or challenging relationship with someone. To the extent you shine a light on those things about the person that you do (or did) appreciate, you can take the focus away from those aspects that are less pleasing.

If you are having challenges with a particular person or relationship, try this: make a list of ten things you appreciate about this person—and/or your relationship—and why. Every person has *some* redeeming qualities so start there. What *do* you like about this person? What can you appreciate about your interactions? What have you learned from this person?

For example, Zoe had a prickly relationship with her cousin John. They were never on the same wavelength. She saw him as a slick salesman who hid behind a fairly thick, false facade. It was particularly irritating to her whenever he boasted or stretched the truth. She loathed the awkward dynamics whenever she encountered him at family gatherings. She used Gratitude to diffuse the tension between them:

> *I'm thankful John is very good about keeping in touch with our grandparents because they savor the attention he gives them—and it takes the pressure off the rest of us.*
>
> *I'm grateful that John is generous because he can be counted on to give to charity, no matter what cause my kids are promoting.*
>
> *I'm grateful that John travels so much because he is a role model for how I'd like to be living.*
>
> *I appreciate John's business success because he is a master in a world I don't understand and because he shares his expertise with the family, which has been especially helpful for our relatives.*
>
> *I'm grateful to understand that John's false bravado comes from a place of low self-esteem because it makes me feel more compassion for him—and less irritation.*
>
> *I'm grateful John is so verbal because there is never a conversational lull when he's around.*

I'm grateful that John so adores his wife and children because it is beautiful to witness and to have as a role model in our family.

It may be challenging to detect positive aspects of a challenging relationship, but to the extent you do, you can begin to shift your perspective about the person and the relationship. We all have weaknesses and failings just as we all have strengths and assets. If you can balance your awareness of the former with your appreciation of the latter, it will be easier to improve the tone and tenor of the relationship.

Remember, the idea of using Life Levers like Gratitude is to start to nudge things to change for the better. Any small improvement is progress. Aim for an "improved" relationship, rather than a "perfect" relationship.

ACTIVITY

Think of a difficult or challenging relationship you have with someone. Make a list of things for which you are grateful about this person.

USING GRATITUDE TO COUNTER PERFECTIONISM AND JUDGMENT

Are you picky? Do you have sky-high standards? Are you hard on yourself (and others)? If so, you might just be a perfectionist. If you tend to be dissatisfied with things not being "good enough" or if you find yourself constantly evaluating, assessing, or otherwise judging your experiences, your efforts, and everyone else, Gratitude can be very helpful indeed.

Whenever things don't seem quite up to snuff, or whenever you are viewing yourself, someone, or something unfavorably, pause and apply Gratitude.

For example, when Mario was dissatisfied with a restaurant meal, he invoked Gratitude to generate alternative thoughts:

> *Well, the food could be better, but I'm grateful to have the opportunity to have a meal with my friends because I enjoy spending time with them.*
>
> *I'm grateful to have the money to go to a restaurant because many people don't. I'm thankful I have a discerning palate because I usually eat tasty food.*
>
> *I'm grateful that someone else prepared my meal so I didn't have to, and I could focus on my conversation with my friends.*
>
> *I'm thankful for this reminder to appreciate my favorite restaurants more.*

Gratitude can nudge you to view any situation as slightly better than your first snap judgment. This can alleviate your disappointment a smidge. This can take a bit of pressure off yourself and those around you.

RECOMMENDED READING

If you'd like to learn more about Gratitude, I recommend M. J. Ryan's seminal book *Attitude of Gratitude*.

Also, Rhonda Byrne's book *The Magic* offers dozens of practical gratitude activities.

For a comprehensive program to overcome perfectionism, check out my book on the topic: *Overcoming Perfectionism: Solutions for Perfectionists*.

CHAPTER 5

Forgiveness is a Highly Effective Life Lever

© *Lisa Rothstein, www.LisaRothstein.com*

Forgiveness is a very powerful Life Lever. Forgiving someone is a small act that can resolve conflicts, heal relationships, and transform enemies into allies. It can dissolve grudges, resentments, guilt, shame, and blame. When you forgive someone, you help heal them, yourself, and the situation.

Applying this lever to yourself is a small act that has even greater consequences. When you forgive yourself, you can resolve issues and release unhelpful patterns of thinking and behaving. If you are seeking self-improvement or wanting to operate more effectively, forgiving yourself is key to real personal growth and development.

◆

WHAT CAN FORGIVENESS DO?

Whenever you sincerely forgive yourself and/or others, you have the opportunity to

- resolve conflicts
- improve relationships
- release grudges and resentments
- overcome regrets, disappointments, and past mistakes
- dissolve guilt, blame, and shame
- disrupt unhealthy or unhelpful thought patterns
- disrupt unhealthy or unhelpful behavior patterns
- feel better about yourself
- accept things you cannot change

◆

FORGIVING OTHERS

Think about your own experience of forgiving someone. There is a visceral release of bad feelings you've harbored against this person. There is a sense of relief. There is a new, more positive feeling towards them. There is a palpable improvement in the relationship.

Remember a time you were forgiven. Recall your gratitude at

being able to get past something you regretted. Think about the release of the burden you were bearing.

Mechanically, Forgiveness is easy. You simply do it.

In practice, it can be more challenging because our clever minds want to protect us from further harm. When someone hurts us, our protective brains want to hold the other person accountable. But Forgiveness is not approval for what occurred. Forgiveness is not "letting someone off the hook". Forgiveness is an acknowledgement that we all make mistakes.

"But you don't understand," you may protest. "They were wrong! They hurt me badly! Why should I forgive them?" Well, ask yourself this: would you rather be right or would you rather be healed? If you want to heal, you must forgive them.

Consider the story of Bill Pelke, a retired Alaskan steelworker. Four teenage girls murdered his grandmother in 1985. Initially, when the fifteen-year-old ringleader, Paula Cooper, was sentenced to die in the electric chair, Bill approved. Subsequently, he underwent a spiritual transformation. He prayed for love and compassion for Paula and her family. He not only forgave her, he led an international crusade on her behalf to remove her from death row. As a result, Paula's sentence was commuted from death by electric chair to sixty years.

Bill went on to co-found a non-profit organization *Journey of Hope... From Violence to Healing* (www.journeyofhope.org)—an international group of "death row family members, family members of the executed, death row survivors, activists and friends" who work to promote non-violence and Forgiveness. As an alternative to the death penalty, they promote "restorative justice"—a process that fosters "offender accountability and the opportunity for the offender to make things right with the victim as much as possible."

If Bill Pelke can forgive the woman who killed his beloved grandmother, is it possible for you to forgive the person who caused you harm?

Truthfully, Forgiveness is letting YOU off the hook. It's a way to release the pain, the anger, the fear, and the resentment you experience when someone hurts you. Forgiveness gives you the opportunity to heal and move on.

Besides, the alternatives don't work. Lashing back or seeking revenge is never as satisfying as you imagine. Harsh actions injure you in the long run. Holding grudges and hard feelings against those who have harmed you hurts you much more than it affects them.

The longer you let resentments fester, the more you are damaging your own happiness. It's impossible to be happy if you are bearing burdens from the past. Who does it serve if you are walking around, bitter and seething about something that happened a decade ago…while the person who hurt you can't even remember your name, let alone the incident? Grudges hurt you, not them.

"But it's too late," you may say. No, it isn't. When you hurt someone, it's better to apologize immediately, of course. But it's better to apologize late than not at all. Similarly, you can be way overdue when it comes to forgiving others. But as soon as you do, you can heal. And you can't truly move forward until you forgive.

"But I don't even know where they are, what they're doing, if they are even alive," you might counter. It doesn't matter. If you can forgive someone in person, it's powerful. But you can also forgive someone without them knowing anything about it. It doesn't matter where they are or what they're doing—you have the power to forgive them, right here, right now.

Forgiveness is really a gift you give yourself. You'll feel the difference in your own heart when you truly forgive someone. There's a little shift, deep down. There is a sensation of release as the burden begins to lift. It feels like relief. It's the first step to replacing the pain of the incident with peace and joy.

Forgiveness is a very simple, very powerful lever. But sometimes it can be challenging to apply. Many people have found the following activities helpful.

ACTIVITY

What grudges are you holding? Who do you need to forgive? Make a list.

FORGIVENESS ACTIVITY

Clear some uninterrupted time for personal reflection. Pick one person you need to forgive from your list on page 50. With this person in mind, answer the following questions:

1. What grudges are you holding against them?

2. What is it costing you to hold these resentments? How does it make you feel?

3. How do these grudges and resentments affect how you are living your life?

4. How do these grudges and resentments affect the people around you?

5. How do these grudges and resentments affect the person you are holding responsible?

6. What benefits might there be to forgiving this person? How would you feel? How might it improve your life?

7. Imagine this person as a child, helpless and alone. To what extent could you have compassion for them in that circumstance?

8. Recognize that this person is a fallible human being, susceptible to making mistakes like everyone else on the planet, including you. Consider that we all do the best we can at any particular moment, given the skills, knowledge, and understanding we have at that time. We would all like to be forgiven for the mistakes we've made.

9. Consider what this person did. In what ways might you have done something similar? *(E.g., if they lied to you, ask in what ways have you been dishonest in your life?)*

10. Remind yourself that Forgiveness is not approval or justification for what happened.
11. Forgive this person. Take a moment. Acknowledge that they are a fallible human being. View them with compassion and kindness. Decide to forgive them. Act accordingly.

FORGIVING YOURSELF

Now, it's one thing to forgive someone else. But it's quite another to forgive yourself. Many of us are hard on ourselves. We punish ourselves for mistakes we've made. But if we insist on carrying negative experiences from our past, we are needlessly denying ourselves happiness in the present.

We need to forgive ourselves. We deserve to be treated kindly and compassionately—especially by ourselves. As human beings, we all make mistakes. Whatever it is, forgive yourself. You deserve the same courtesy you would give someone else. Imagine the relief of truly forgiving yourself! Picture yourself laying those unnecessary burdens down…and moving forward with your life. Rather than berating yourself for things you can't change, wouldn't you prefer to be spending that energy on something more pleasant, healthy, or helpful?

ACTIVITY

For what do you need to forgive yourself? Make a list.

On page 55 is a Self-forgiveness Activity you can use to work through each item on your list. For best results, pick only one item and answer the questions. Forgive yourself. Wait at least a day until you address another item on your list.

SELF-FORGIVENESS ACTIVITY

Clear some uninterrupted time for private reflection. Pick one item on your list on page 54. Answer the following questions:

1. What does it cost you to carry this burden? How does it affect different areas of your life? Your relationships? Your attitude?

2. What does it cost others around you?

3. What benefits would there be to forgiving yourself? How would you feel? How would it change how you are living your life?

4. What's been stopping you from forgiving yourself? Why are you denying yourself this relief?

5. What needs to happen for you to forgive yourself?

6. Take a moment. Acknowledge that you are a fallible human, that you make mistakes (like we all make mistakes), and that you deserve Forgiveness for them. Consider that you do the best you can at any particular moment, given your skills and understanding at that time. View yourself with compassion and kindness. See yourself as a small child. Forgive yourself.

CHAPTER 6

Mindfulness is a Highly Effective Life Lever

© Lisa Rothstein, www.LisaRothstein.com

Mindfulness is perhaps the subtlest and most mysterious Life Lever. At some level it seems "too easy" to make any sort of difference. Yet somehow it does. Somehow, Mindfulness is a highly effective Lever for reducing stress, overcoming procrastination, getting things done, improving relationships, and more.

For our purposes, there are two main types of Mindfulness: Focus and Meditation.

Focus is a matter of doing one thing at a time and giving it your full attention.

Meditation can be as simple as taking a two- or three-minute break for a quiet, thought-free pause.

Many people avoid or resist applying this Lever because they expect it to be boring and/or excruciating and/or ineffective. Those who actually implement it find it life-changing. I encourage you try it for yourself to see how it affects you.

◆

MINDFULNESS AS FOCUS

If you want to do more, do less. If you want to get more done, do only one thing at a time. If you want to be more effective or efficient, give whatever you're doing your full attention.

It doesn't matter how many projects, activities, and ideas you are juggling.

At a given instant, you can only do one thing.

"Oh no, not me," you may insist. "I'm a multi-tasker. Right now, while I'm reading this, I'm also designing a new product line, listening to the news, and texting my mom."

You may believe you are doing several things simultaneously but studies have shown that's not possible. Really what happens is that your brain is toggling among those different activities every second or so. At any given instant, you are doing only one of them. Every time you switch tasks, there is a cognitive cost as your brain switches gears. (*Now where was I again?*) By toggling so quickly among different activities, you're not doing any of them particularly well. Research has proven that multi-taskers reduce their productivity by about forty percent. Forty percent!

Frankly, you're being unnecessarily hard on yourself. It's much easier to focus on one thing at a time. And here's the good news: when you stop trying to do everything at the same instant—when you focus on just one activity at a time—you will get more done, faster, more easily, with less stress.

Let me repeat that—on the off chance you're, say, texting a friend, jotting down a grocery list, and watching a show or movie while you're reading this.

◆

SEVEN BENEFITS OF FOCUSING ON ONE THING AT A TIME

1. It's easier.
2. You'll get more done.
3. You'll get things done faster.
4. You'll get things done more easily.
5. You'll reduce stress.
6. You'll feel better.
7. You'll be more pleasant to be around.

◆

HOW TO FOCUS

Just do one thing at time. Give the task your full attention. That's it. When you conclude one activity, pick the next task and do it.

Go on. Try it. Right now. As you read, resist anything that is competing for your attention.

The more you can limit your focus to one and only one thing at a time, the better.

If, however, you find it difficult to concentrate, take a moment to identify and curtail whatever distractions are interfering with your attention.

Sarah is easily sidetracked by any notifications of new emails or new social media posts. Jason is easily distracted by the need to research. Even minor decisions will set him running to Google the options, which often lead to him surfing random topics unrelated to the task at hand.

When I am writing, my attention can be hijacked by ideas and "To Do's". My brain suddenly starts churning out thoughts about article topics, or things I need to add to the shopping list, or phone calls I need to make. My solution is to have a "Park it Pad" next to me when I work. When ideas pop up that are unrelated to the task at hand, I jot them down, "parking" them to be dealt with later.

What interrupts your focus? Be candid. Is it email? The phone? Internet surfing? The piles of half-done projects piled around you? Your "To Do" list(s)? Any of the thousand apps on your device? Other people?

Take a moment to write down what tends to interfere with you sticking to one thing at a time. Next, brainstorm ways to remove or reduce those temptations. For example, you might schedule specific time periods to check your email or to return phone calls. You might postpone your internet surfing or Facebook time until the conclusion of your workday.

Yes, I realize you need to be able to receive and respond to texts from family members and you can't schedule when your client will call with an urgent request. Of course, it's impossible to eliminate all distractions all the time. But to the extent you can *reduce* distractions—especially the siren calls of the internet and social media—the more you will reap the benefits of focusing on one thing at a time.

Life Levers • 61

ACTIVITY	
List your favorite distractions. What tends to interfere with your focus?	For each, brainstorm ways to reduce or remove each of these distractions, given your personal situation and preferences. What's worked well for you in the past? What have you noticed works well for others? What else might you try?

If distractions are an ongoing challenge for you, meditation may be a solution. Meditation is basically training your mind to ignore distracting thoughts and to focus on the task at hand. It's a way to teach your brain to do what you want, when you want… rather than being at the mercy of random thoughts whenever they occur to you.

MINDFULNESS AS MEDITATION

The psychological and physiological benefits of meditation are many and profound. Besides improving your focus, meditation is a proven stress reducer. Almost every bodily system functions better when you meditate regularly. Meditation has been proven to be an effective remedy for low mood, depression, and anxiety. For many, meditation is also a spiritual practice that has brought solace, comfort, and meaning to its practitioners.

◆

THE MEDITATION MYTH

Despite all the potential benefits of meditation, what often stops people from giving it a whirl is the misconception that meditation requires grueling, boring and/or inconvenient l-o-n-g sessions. The truth is that you can derive all the psychological and physiological benefits of meditation through very brief (two- or three-minute) sessions, sprinkled through your day.

In fact, according to meditation guru Yongey Mingyur Rinpoche, it's better to aim for very short mini-meditation sessions than to tackle longer sessions.

How convenient! We've got a lot going on. It's easy enough to take a two- or three-minute meditation break between tasks.

It's not difficult. It's not complicated. It's just a matter of doing it. If we actually take a few brief meditation breaks every day, we will experience cognitive and health benefits.

◆

MEDITATION BASICS

The basic concept is to devote some time to quieting your mind. There is no wrong way to meditate. Avoid beating yourself up if your mind drifts or ideas pop up when you're meditating. Whatever happens during your meditation period is perfect. There are a thousand different ways to meditate. Here are some basic techniques:

SAMPLE MEDITATION TECHNIQUES

1. Set a timer for two or three minutes. Sit upright. Close your eyes and focus on your breathing. Concentrate on the air entering and leaving your body. When your attention drifts, gently bring it back to your breathing.
2. Set a timer for two or three minutes. Sit upright and close your eyes. Select a word to repeat to yourself (e.g., "peace" or "love" or "joy" or "om"). When your attention drifts, gently bring it back to your focus word.
3. Select an image on which to concentrate—for example, a beautiful landscape or a piece of art. Set a timer for two or three minutes. Sit upright in front of your chosen image and focus on it. When your attention drifts, gently bring it back to the image.
4. Set a timer for two or three minutes. Sit upright and close your eyes. Clear your mind completely. Try to avoid thinking about anything at all. As thoughts arise, label them as "just thinking" or "just judging" or "just obsessing" and allow them to pass by—like clouds pass through the sky.

5. Set a timer for two or three minutes. Sit upright and close your eyes. Ask, "What do I need to know?" Quiet your mind and listen attentively for an answer.
6. Light a candle. Set a timer for two or three minutes. Sit upright and focus on the candle flame. As thoughts occur to you, gently push them aside and re-focus on the candle flame.
7. Set a timer for ten minutes. Walk slowly and purposefully, putting each foot down slowly and carefully. Direct your attention to your movement. When other ideas intervene, push them gently aside and re-focus on your steps.
8. Set a timer for fifteen minutes. Lie down in a comfortable position. Direct your attention to your left foot. Slowly move your attention to your left ankle for a moment or two. Slowly shift your focus to your left shin, then later your left knee and eventually your left thigh. Repeat with your right leg. Continue the process, moving your attention slowly up through your torso, down each arm, up your neck and through your face and head.
9. Find some guided meditations to try. There are plenty of apps and online options.

Scientific research shows that if you develop a regular practice, meditation can (and will) improve your health and lift your mood. It is likely to enhance other areas of your life as well, however the specific benefits will depend on your unique circumstances and preferences. The only way to learn how meditation will affect you is to try it.

ACTIVITY

1. Make an appointment with yourself for a month from today. Schedule it on your calendar.
2. Take the next month to test any or all of the preceding Meditation techniques. See which work best for you, under what circumstances. Make a point of taking at least two meditation breaks of at least two minutes each, every day for the next thirty days.

3. Every day, put a checkmark or a star on your calendar every time you meditate for at least two minutes.
4. At the end of the month, use your scheduled appointment to ask yourself the following:

- How do I feel, physically?

- What is my general mood these days?

- What differences do I notice? *Consider different areas of your life including your work, your relationships, and your health.*

APPLYING MINDFULNESS AS A LEVER

Among other things, Mindfulness is a highly effective lever for

- getting things done
- overcoming procrastination
- reducing stress, and
- improving relationships.

USING MINDFULNESS TO GET THINGS DONE

Mindfulness is a highly effective Lever for getting things done. If you pick one thing and give it your full attention, you will accomplish more and you will complete things more effectively with less stress.

If you have several competing priorities (and who among us doesn't), assign each task a specific period of your day when you focus on it and only it.

Remember during grade school when you studied different subjects during different periods? In a given morning you might do math problems, then learn some history, then run around the schoolyard for recess, then read a story, then learn some geography. You covered a lot of material by focusing on one topic at a time. You can structure your current day (or week) the same way so that you give attention to everything that needs doing.

For example, right now I'm writing. I'm only writing. My "Park It Pad" is handy. My phones and internet are turned off. Two hours from now, I'll be at the gym, engrossed in following my Zumba teacher's choreography. This afternoon, I'll prepare for my client sessions. During each session, I'll clear everything from my desk except for my client file, a blank writing pad, and a pen. I'll be focused on my client—and only them—until I consolidate my notes after the session concludes. After my appointments are finished, I'll devote an hour to business communications and practicalities. I'll clear my "to do's" and shut down all my tech so when it's family time in the evening, work does not intervene.

On the next page is a process to help you identify and devote specific blocks of time to focus on whatever is important to you.

ACTIVITY

1. What are your top priorities this week?
   -
   -
   -

2. Customize the chart below to sketch out your week (work, play, sleep, etc.).

Time Block	Mon	Tues	Wed	Thurs	Fri	Sat	Sun

3. Designate at least one time period for each of your top priorities.
4. Prior to each of these designated blocks of time, remove or reduce possible distractions. Commence these designated times mindfully. Make a point of actually devoting these blocks of time to the priority you specified—and only that priority.

USING MINDFULNESS TO OVERCOME PROCRASTINATION

If you find yourself procrastinating by not doing some particular task, you can use Mindfulness to move forward.

A timer is a wonderful way to foster or jump-start Mindfulness. There is something about a sudden time constraint that seems to marshal our attention. If you are procrastinating or otherwise hesitating to do something, set a timer for ten minutes. Commit to doing as much as possible during those ten minutes. Whatever you get done is enough.

Bonus #1: You will be surprised how much you can accomplish when you give yourself a ten-minute time limit.

Bonus #2: Odds are good that when the timer goes off, you won't want to stop. As we have discussed in Chapter 2, a body in motion stays in motion. Sometimes we just need a little nudge to break out of our inertia. In this case, the timer is a tool to kick start Mindfulness which will prod you past the Tipping Point and get you going.

ACTIVITY

What's a task you really should do, but have been putting off?
   Commit to devoting ten minutes to this task, right now.
   Set a timer for ten minutes and give your undivided attention to the task at hand.

USING MINDFULNESS TO REDUCE STRESS

Many studies have demonstrated the high toll of stress physically, psychologically, emotionally, and interpersonally. Thankfully, Mindfulness is a highly effective remedy for stress.

The first step in reducing stress is to be aware when it occurs. Many people don't understand how stress affects them. To what extent are you attentive to your own stress level? What do you notice when you experience stress? What are the warning signs?

ACTIVITY

Think of a time you were under stress. How did it affect you?

What did it feel like, physically?

What did if feel like, emotionally?

What else did you notice?

What impact did your stress have on other people around you?

When you experience a stressful situation or find yourself feeling overwhelmed, pause and focus. Ask yourself: What is one thing I can do now that will make a difference?

You can't do everything so just pick something—anything—and do that. Focus on that and that alone.

You are apt to find that taking mindful action immediately reduces stress and feelings of being overwhelmed. Action—especially focused, mindful action—will give you instant relief and direct your actions more productively.

> ## ACTIVITY
>
> What's on your mind? What's causing you stress today?
>
> Make a list of specific actions you could take right now that would make a difference. What might shift things?
>
>
>
>
>
> Choose one item on your list. (If in doubt, pick the simplest, easiest thing you could do.)
>
> Do it. Focus on this task and only this task.

In some cases, there may be no apparent concrete act you can take to change the situation. In these instances, your most effective course of action might be to "accept the things you cannot change." Find peace with it…otherwise you'll make yourself miserable.

Acceptance isn't always easy, but if something is unchangeable, it may be the only healthy, mindful option you have at the present time.

Here's an activity to use Mindfulness to help you manage an unchangeable situation.

MINDFULNESS TOOL: ACCEPTING CIRCUMSTANCES

1. Pause. Reflect. Take stock of how the situation is affecting you.
   - How does it make you feel?
   - What thoughts does it elicit?
   - How does it make you behave?
   - What is it costing you?

2. How can you reframe the situation to be more bearable?
   What is the bigger picture? Is this situation temporary? What is the objective reality? Might some good come out of the situation eventually? How significant is this situation, in the grand scheme of things? To what more important priorities could you give your attention?

3. Identify and take any actions you can that will minimize the impact of this situation on you.
   - What can you do to make things more palatable?

- What can you do to distract yourself?

- What support do you have? To whom can you turn for wisdom, guidance, and/or solace?

- To what extent are others affected by the situation? What support can you provide them?

4. Take a moment. Accept the situation.

USING MINDFULNESS TO IMPROVE RELATIONSHIPS

Mindfulness is a guaranteed way to improve and deepen relationships of every kind—professional and personal. When you give people your full attention when you're interacting with them, you are strengthening the bonds between you. You are signaling that they matter and that what they have to say matters.

Consider what it's like when you're having lunch with someone and they spend half the meal checking their phone, texting other people, and jumping around topics that have little to do with your part of the conversation. Think about when you call a colleague and you can hear them clicking away on their keyboard. You know their typing has little to do with the topic you are trying to discuss with them because they repeatedly say something like, "Sorry, what was that? What were you saying?"

Compare that with your experience of someone giving you their full attention. When someone really listens—when they take in what you say—it's validating. It makes you feel like you matter to the other person—or that the topic you wish to discuss matters.

When you apply Mindfulness to a relationship it means you are making this person the priority right now. It means that when you are interacting with them, you focus on what they are communicating. It means you listen attentively. Mindfulness signals to the other person that they matter and/or what they have to say matters.

Try it. When you are mindful with your romantic partner, you draw closer. When you are mindful with your friends, family members, neighbors, and acquaintances, you strengthen those bonds. When you are mindful with a client, colleague, boss, or stakeholder, you validate them and you rise in their esteem.

It can be as simple as giving someone your undivided attention during a conversation. Focus on understanding what they are saying, rather than thinking about what you plan to say next. Avoid interrupting. Ask questions of clarification.

ACTIVITY	
What relationships would you like to improve? Make a list.	For each person, list ways you could be more mindful during your interactions.

RECOMMENDED READING

If you'd like to learn more about Meditation, here are some wonderful books:

Wherever You Go, There You Are by Jon Kabat-Zinn

Lovingkindness by Sharon Salzberg

Joy of Living by Yongey Mingyur Rinpoche

Peace is in Every Step by Thich Nhat Hanh, Arnold Kotler and H. H. The Dalai Lama

For more about using Meditation to heal depression: *The Mindful Way Through Depression: Freeing Yourself from Chronic Unhappiness* by Mark William, John Teasdale, Zindel Segal, and Jon Kabat-Zinn. (This book comes with a CD of guided meditations.)

CHAPTER 7

Using Life Levers to Solve a Problem

© *Lisa Rothstein, www.LisaRothstein.com*

In this chapter, the Life Lever Approach is expanded with a Preparation Step. This enhanced process will be applied to solve a problem, address a challenge, or alleviate a burden.

Everyone has at least one problem in their life. What challenge is front and center for you right now? Use the steps in this chapter to identify and apply Life Levers to solve it.

Begin by examining your current situation. Specifically, what is your problem? What are the thoughts, feelings, words, and deeds you are currently experiencing during this challenge?

The more specific you can be about what your problem is and its effects on you, the easier it is to discover possible solutions.

For example, it's one thing to wail, "I'm drowning in debt". Okay, you've stated that you have a big problem but you're giving yourself no clues as to what exactly is going on, let alone how to improve things. So, you're in debt. Be specific. How much do you owe? How is it affecting you? What actions are you taking? Notice the difference between the first sentence in the paragraph and this description:

> *I owe the credit card company $25,000, which is scary, frustrating, and embarrassing. I'm afraid I'll never pay it off, and yet I'm still spending more than I'm making. Paying off the minimum payment every month is not reducing the amount I owe. Instead, the number keeps growing because of the interest charges and fees. Avoiding my bills doesn't help. I'm stuck and don't know how to break the cycle.*

The more you can be specific about the thoughts, feelings, words, and deeds that comprise the problem, the easier it becomes to identify possible Levers that will start to shift things for you, given your unique circumstances and preferences. That's why only you can devise an appropriate solution. Only you are fully aware of everything going on in your life and how you prefer to operate. Ten people with the same problem might solve it in ten different ways using ten different Levers.

The question is: What will work for you? To figure this out, it's helpful to add a Preparation Step to the Life Lever Approach we introduced in Chapter 2. This supplementary phase features a structured series of questions designed to help you tease apart the components of whatever problem is a priority for you right now.

PREPARATION STEP: EXAMINE YOUR CURRENT SITUATION

This supplementary phase is designed to

- enhance your understanding of the situation
- expand your perspective
- generate more options for possible Levers that will work, given your unique circumstances and preferences.

Clear some uninterrupted time for personal reflection. For best results, I encourage you to write out your responses. As soon as you begin documenting your answers, new information and insights will occur to you. The more information you capture, the more options you'll have for moving forward.

1. State the problem. *Be as specific as possible.*

2. How do I feel about this problem? What emotions am I experiencing in this situation? *Answer in as much detail as possible.*

TROUBLESHOOTING

If you need more prompts, complete the following sentence fragments:

I'm sad that...

I'm disappointed...

I'm resentful...

I'm mad because...

I'm upset...

I'm worried...

I'm embarrassed...

I regret...

I'm hurt...

I'm afraid...

I don't like...

I'm frustrated that...

I'm annoyed by...

I hate...

I feel...

3. What do I think about this problem? What are my thoughts about the situation? *Jot down your responses in as much detail as possible.*

> ## TROUBLESHOOTING
>
> If you need more prompts, complete the following sentence fragments:
>
> *It seems...*
>
> *I see that...*
>
> *I understand...*
>
> *I believe...*
>
> *I know...*
>
> *I wonder...*
>
> *I don't know...*
>
> *I need...*
>
> *I want...*
>
> *I don't want...*
>
> *I think...*

Whatever problems we have loom large in our minds. It's natural to exaggerate the size and scope of things. An important step in solving a problem is to evaluate the situation accurately.

For example, let's say one of your thoughts is, "It seems impossible to get out of debt." If you examine this statement more closely, you can question its accuracy and validity. You can consider evidence to the contrary. You can re-write it to be more accurate.

In this example, you might revise your original statement to something like this:

It might be challenging to get out of debt but it is possible. I know this because other people have done it. There are many ways to earn more, to spend less, and to pay down debt. If other people can get out of debt, it's possible for me to do so, too. I need to figure out what will work for me, given my circumstances.

---

4. Go back through each response you gave to questions 2 and 3. For each item, consider the following:

   - Is this accurate?
   - Is this true?
   - Is this valid?
   - Is there evidence that proves it?
   - Is there evidence that disproves it?
   - What are the facts here?

Revise your answers to reflect what is actually true.
Cross out what is untrue.
Change your wording to more accurately reflect the situation.

It's also helpful to review your original statement of the problem to see if any wording changes start to shift things towards a solution.

Using the debt example, the original statement of the problem on page 76 might be rephrased to something like this:

I owe the credit card company $25,000 which is scary, frustrating, and embarrassing. I would feel so much better if I owed less. It is possible for me to pay down my debt. I need to learn effective ways to improve my financial situation that are practical for me to implement given my life circumstances.

Life Levers • 81

5. Once you have re-written your answers to be accurate and truthful, consider any discrepancies between the objective situation and how you have been describing your problem until now.

   - Read your original description of the problem (on page 77).
   - Going forward, what change in words or framing could you make that might improve the situation? Be specific. Revise your statement of the problem accordingly.

6. Next, ask: How are my actions contributing to the problem?
   Answer in as much detail as possible.

> ### TROUBLESHOOTING
>
> If you need more prompts, complete the following sentence fragments:
>
> *I've been...*
>
> *I'm doing...*
>
> *I'm trying...*
>
> *I'm...*
>
> *I'm not...*
>
> *I'm avoiding...*

STEP ONE: CHOOSE A TINY CHANGE AS YOUR LEVER

> Review everything you wrote in your Preparation Step. As you do, circle or highlight any key insights about your problem.
>
> Given all this, what tiny change in thought, word, feeling, or deed can you make that might start to shift the situation? *Make a list.*
>
>
>
>
>
>
>
> Review your list and pick something—anything—as your Lever. Circle it. Proceed to Step Two.

TROUBLESHOOTING

If you had difficulty making a list of possible changes, list answers to any or all of the following questions:

- How might a child solve this problem?

- How might an alien from another planet solve this problem?

- How might a politician solve this problem?

- How might a teenager solve this problem?

- How might an artist solve this problem?

- How might your grandparent solve this problem?

- How might a teacher solve this problem?

- How might a scientist solve this problem?

- What about this problem is funny? Ironic?

Review your answers. As you do, ask how could this response be adapted to work in your situation? *Circle or highlight anything that seems useful.*

Given all this, what tiny change in thought, word, feeling, or deed can you make that might start to shift the situation?

Pick something—anything—as your Lever. Proceed to Step Two.

STEP TWO: START

Beginning right now, implement the tiny change you chose in Step One.

Proceed to Step Three.

TROUBLESHOOTING

If you find yourself hesitating to get started, refer to the troubleshooting techniques listed for Step Two in Chapter 3.

STEP THREE: CARRY ON. MONITOR AND ADJUST ACCORDINGLY

MONITOR YOUR PROGRESS

A. Keep Track

- What are simple, easy ways you can track your progress in solving your problem?

B. Analyze and Adjust

Every few days ask yourself:

- To what extent am I doing what I intended?
- What differences do I notice?
- What adjustments need to be made, if any?

At a minimum, check in once a week.

Seek small, consistent shifts in your desired direction. Be kind to yourself. Praise any forward momentum. Your goal is to aim for progress, rather than perfection. After a few weeks, see what consequences you notice.

C. Progress Check

Schedule an appointment with yourself for a month from now. On that date, pause to answer the following:

- Overall, how are you doing, compared with how you were when you started?

- What differences do you notice?

- Going forward, what adjustments are needed, if any?

D. Adjust Accordingly

If you are experiencing progress towards solving your problem, carry on.

Adjust as necessary. When it seems like you should do more or less, do so. If it's time to switch Levers, do so.

TROUBLESHOOTING

If you have difficulty monitoring your progress and/or making adjustments, refer to the techniques listed for Step Three in Chapter 3.

♦

This chapter examined how adding a Preparation Step enhances the Life Lever Approach when it is applied to solving a problem. Variations of this process can be used to accomplish something specific or to improve your life more generally. The next two chapters explain how.

CHAPTER 8

Using Life Levers to Accomplish Something

© Lisa Rothstein, www.LisaRothstein.com

Just as the Life Lever Approach can help you solve a problem, it can also help you accomplish something. Do you have a particular task, goal, or dream you'd like to achieve? This might be something you've already started working towards or something you haven't yet begun. If so, you can work through the activities in this chapter to make it happen. (Otherwise feel free to skip ahead to the next chapter.)

Whatever it is you'd like to accomplish, the key here is to think small.

◆

BABY STEPS

No matter how big the task at hand, to the extent you can break it down into tiny components, the easier it can be accomplished. As the Tao Te Ching proverb says, "A journey of a thousand miles begins with a single step."

For example, "buying a home" is an overwhelming, scary, exciting, and complex project. To achieve it, it's helpful to cleave it into smaller tasks such as budgeting, saving the down payment, identifying priorities for your family's needs, researching options, finding a great realtor, reviewing homes for sale, making the offer, arranging financing, arranging utilities and insurance, moving, etc.

Each of these elements can be further broken down into smaller pieces. For example, "researching options" might involve exploring different neighborhoods, gathering relevant information about each (home prices, crime rates, local schools, walkability, local amenities, transportation considerations, etc.), reviewing listings online, and going to some open houses to learn about the local realty market.

By slicing each of these tasks into even smaller pieces, you can identify tiny changes that are doable. "Reviewing listings online" might translate into "spending at least fifteen minutes a day looking at online real estate listings, at least four days a week". With this formula, you are guaranteed to spend at least an hour a week on something that is important to your family and your goal of owning a new home.

Ideally, Baby Steps should be laughably small. So small you don't think twice about doing them. That's the whole point. When what's on your "To Do" list is really, truly easy, you'll do it.

With Baby Steps in mind, let's apply the Life Levers Approach to accomplishing your chosen task, goal, dream, or desired outcome.

PREPARATION STEP: EXAMINE YOUR CURRENT SITUATION

The Preparation Step introduced in Chapter 7 is beneficial here, but not mandatory. If you are raring to go ahead with your task, by all means feel free to skip ahead to Step 1. However, you may find the Preparation Step helpful if:

- you find yourself hesitating to start
- you wonder why you've never taken steps towards this project before, or
- you have taken steps towards your goal but your progress became blocked or derailed

For example, imagine that your dream is to climb Mount Kilimanjaro. It's been on your Bucket List since you were a teen and yet you've never taken any action towards actually doing it. By going through the process detailed in the Preparation Step, you can examine the thoughts and emotions you have about the enterprise so you can understand what's been hampering your progress...and how to move forward. You might discover that any possible concerns are easily addressable once you know what they are.

Or you may find that when you stop and think about it, you don't really want to climb Mount Kilimanjaro at this point in your life. Perhaps you want to do some more moderate hiking, closer to home. Or maybe instead you want a different sort of adventure—a safari, say, or an Alaskan cruise, or maybe a camping trip with your family. Great. Easy enough to reframe your goal accordingly and make it happen.

Begin by defining exactly what you want to accomplish. The more specific you can be about your desires, the better. "I wanna travel" generates some options for proceeding, but they will be fewer, vaguer, less compelling, and less motivating than a more specific goal such as, "I want to climb Mount Kilimanjaro within five years."

The more specific your goal, the easier it is to detect which Levers may be effective, given your unique circumstance and preferences.

1. State your task, goal, dream, or desired accomplishment. Be as specific as possible.

Next, it's important to identify your motivation. **Why** do you want to accomplish this goal?

For example, many of us set a goal of losing ten pounds. Most of us don't succeed because our true motivation isn't compelling enough to make us actually exercise and restrict our food consumption.

It's one thing to say "I'd like to lose ten pounds because my jeans are too tight." It's something completely different to say, "My doctor says I'm overweight and putting undue strain on my heart. I must lose ten pounds within the next two months because my health is at risk and until I lose weight, I am more likely to have a cardiac arrest." Which rationale is more compelling? Which will lead to real progress in losing weight?

The key here is to be candid. Why do you *really* want to do this thing? Consider the extent to which your real motivation is compelling to you. If your true rationale seems flimsy, pause and ask yourself if you really want to do this thing. If not, congratulate yourself. You just saved yourself a lot of time and effort by avoiding a project that you really did not want to do at this point in time. You might someday, but for now, park it. Pick a different goal and return to question 1.

---

2. Review your goal statement. Why do you want to accomplish this?

   Be candid. Why do you *really* want to accomplish this thing?

   To what extent is your rationale compelling enough that you will move forward? Do you really want to do this thing at this point in time?
   If yes, please proceed with this process.
   If no, select a different goal and return to question 1.

Next, consider any and all emotions you have regarding this goal. Using our Kilimanjaro example, for example:

> *I'm excited by the idea of visiting Africa for the first time. It feels so exotic!*
> *I'm yearning for an adventure.*
> *I love to travel and I haven't done as much as I'd like.*
> *I'm worried about getting sick.*
> *I'm worried if I have the physical strength necessary to make the trip.*
> *It would be so cool to actually climb a mountain, let alone Kilimanjaro! It'd be such a high!*
> *I'd love to see the snows of Kilimanjaro while they still exist.*

3. How do you feel about your goal? What emotions does this goal elicit?
   Answer in as much detail as possible.

> ## TROUBLESHOOTING
>
> If you need more prompts, complete the following sentence fragments:
>
> *I'm nervous about...*
>
> *I'm excited about...*
>
> *I'm concerned...*
>
> *I'm happy...*
>
> *I'm worried...*
>
> *I like...*
>
> *I don't like...*
>
> *I love...*
>
> *I feel...*

Now, turn your attention to any and all thoughts you have about this goal. Using the Kilimanjaro example:

> *I know I have enough vacation days available.*
> *I don't know how much it would cost or if I can afford it.*
> *I have many logistical questions. Where would I fly? How would I get to the mountain? What gear would I need? What health precautions or vaccinations are necessary? Should I get travel insurance?*
> *I'm not a mountain climber or an athlete but lots of people like me have climbed Kilimanjaro, so I believe it's possible. I don't know what training I'd need or how I would get it.*

4. What do you think about this goal? What are your underlying beliefs about this goal? What facts do you know to be true? What questions do you have? *Jot down your responses in as much detail as possible.*

TROUBLESHOOTING

If you need more prompts, complete the following sentence fragments:

It seems...

I see that...

I understand...

I believe...

I know...

I wonder...

I don't know...

I need...

I want...

I don't want...

I need to learn...

Next, it's helpful to pause and examine the words you are using to describe the opportunity.

Using the Kilimanjaro example, you might have some excitement about the possible adventure as well as some specific concerns and challenges. If this were your goal, it would be up to you to decide what these elements mean to you, given your unique circumstances and preferences.

---

5. Now go back through your responses to questions 2, 3 and 4. Circle the words that jump out at you. What do you notice?

6. Review your goal statement (on page 91).
   - Is it accurate?
   - What adjustments need to be made?
   - Going forward, what change in words or framing might help your progress towards what you really want to accomplish?

7. Rewrite your goal statement accordingly.

The last part of the preparation step is to examine your current situation. Specifically, what are you now doing that is furthering your goal—and what are you now doing that is hampering your progress.

For example:

> *I'm now thinking about the pragmatics of such a trip, including what it would entail and what it would mean for my family.*

> *I'm identifying information I need, such as travel options, costs, health precautions, travel insurance, training options, and gear requirements.*
>
> *Until I actually start researching options, I'm not doing much to move this forward.*
>
> *I'm avoiding the research.*
>
> *I'm avoiding having a conversation with my spouse about a possible trip.*

---

8. What are you now doing that is furthering what you want to accomplish?

9. What are you now doing that is hampering your progress?

STEP ONE: CHOOSE A TINY CHANGE AS YOUR LEVER

If you have skipped over the Preparation Step, take a moment to state your desired goal, task, or dream. Write it down. Be as specific as possible.

If you have done the Preparation Step, review your answers. Next, answer the following questions.

What tiny change in feeling might improve my progress towards my goal?

What tiny change in thinking/thought/belief might improve my progress?

What tiny change in words/framing might improve my progress?

What tiny change in behavior might improve my progress?

Review your lists and pick something—anything—as your Lever. Proceed to Step Two.

> ### TROUBLESHOOTING
>
> If you had difficulty making a list of possible changes, list answers to the following questions:
>
> - What's the easiest thing I could do to move things forward?
>
> - What's something laughably tiny I could do that might move things forward?
>
> Pick something—anything—as your Lever. Proceed to Step Two.

◆

STEP TWO: START

Beginning right now, implement the small change you chose in Step One.

Proceed to Step Three.

> ### TROUBLESHOOTING
>
> If you find yourself hesitating to get started, refer to the troubleshooting techniques listed for Step Two in Chapter 3.

STEP THREE: CARRY ON. MONITOR AND ADJUST ACCORDINGLY

When aiming to accomplish something, it is of vital importance that you allow yourself a regular opportunity to do what you intend. If you intend to spend fifteen minutes a day researching your trip, make a point of doing so and monitor your progress. The more often, and the more consistently, you take tiny steps to move forward, the more likely you are to succeed.

MONITOR YOUR PROGRESS

A. Keep Track

- What are simple, easy ways you can track your progress?

B. Analyze and Adjust

Every few days ask yourself:

- To what extent am I doing what I intended?
- What differences do I notice?
- What adjustments need to be made, if any?

At a minimum check in once a week.

C. Progress Check

Schedule an appointment with yourself for a month from now. On that date, pause to answer the following:

- Overall, how are you doing, compared with how you were when you started?

- What progress do you notice? Are you closer to your goal?

- What challenges need to be addressed?

- Going forward, what adjustments are needed, if any?

D. Adjust Accordingly

If you are experiencing progress towards your goal, carry on.

If adjustments are needed, do what makes sense. When it seems like you should do more or less, do so. If it's time to switch Levers, do so.

THE MAGIC HOUR METHOD

In my experience as a coach and a consultant, I've found that many people have trouble giving themselves permission to actually spend time on their goal or dream. For example, Mike loves playing guitar and aspires to play in a local band…but he feels guilty when he takes time away from his family to practice. Susan wants to patent a business idea she has…but keeps deferring for random reasons.

If you find yourself not giving yourself time to do what you actually want to do, consider my Magic Hour technique. It's very simple: Devote an hour a day to pursue your goal or dream.

You'd be amazed at what you can accomplish in sixty minutes a day—and how fast sixty daily minutes can yield substantial progress. Using the Magic Hour Method, I've launched a website, written twenty books, honed my dance skills, automated my jewelry production, become more fit, upped my weekly reading quota, deepened my spiritual practices, fostered my dogs' obedience skills, de-cluttered my entire house, organized my photos, and crossed dozens of random items off my "To Do Someday" list.

My coaching clients have accomplished even more using this technique.

I'd wager that you can accomplish ANYTHING in an hour a day. Yes, you can find that new home. Yes, you can launch a local band. Yes, you can patent that product. Yes, you can learn Italian. What's your biggest dream? You can probably accomplish it in an hour a day.

How is that possible? Well, for one thing, "An Hour a Day" means you're actually spending time on your dream project. If you can consistently spend at least sixty daily minutes on the task, you will make steady progress towards your goal, whatever it is.

Second, it's *only* an hour a day. If the project is truly important enough to you, you will find an hour a day to spend on it.

It's also a way of overcoming any guilt. It's only an hour a day. Given everything you have on your plate and all the time you devote to doing things for others, you deserve to give yourself time to do what's important to you. Anyone who loves you wants you to be happy and healthy. Anyone who truly loves you would prefer that you take an hour a day to do what's important to you —instead of having you be resentful or grumpy or miserable or acting like a martyr because you have zero time for yourself.

An hour a day? It's doable. Speaking for myself, I can waste MUCH more than an hour each day doing things that don't really matter—surfing the 'net or watching movies or puttering around the house. I'm happy to replace sixty of those minutes with something that's actually important to me. You can do the same. What is your own biggest time waster? Wouldn't you rather spend it on something that matters to you?

I call this the Magic Hour Method for several reasons.

1. You can accomplish a lot very efficiently

Echoing the whole point of this book: The more tiny steps you take, the more often, the more progress you will see.

2. It helps you focus

"Yikes! I only have an hour to do this thing I really want to do!" Poof! Go typical distractions, excuses, and procrastination.

3. It feels magical

It's freeing and soothing and gratifying to devote your attention to something you care about. It lifts your spirit and generates joy.

4. It enhances other aspects of your life

When you actually give yourself time to devote to what you care about, it gives you energy. You have more oomph to tackle everything else in your life—and you do so with less resentment because you are no longer being a martyr to your responsibilities.

Hey, it's only an hour a day. Why not give it a try and see if it works for you? As you will see, it's really another version of the Life Lever Approach, tweaked for maximum efficiency:

THE MAGIC HOUR METHOD

1. Select a project

Pick something. Anything. What would you like to do?

2. Begin today

Yes, really. What's the first thing you need to do to accomplish this task? Just start doing it.

Work at least an hour on it. By this I mean quality, focused work. No interruptions. No distractions. No shifting gears to other activities.

If it helps, set a timer to keep you on task and focused—get as much as you can get done before the buzzer goes.

3. Keep track

When you complete today's session, pull out your favorite calendar (paper or electronic), On today's date, mark a star, a checkmark or some other sign that you put in at least one hour of quality, focused work.

You can spend more time if you wish—just be sure to keep track of every day that you complete at least an hour on your chosen project.

4. Reward yourself

Do something pleasant, healthy, and easy. Even five minutes outside can be a little boost. Make a list of suitable treats you'd like.

5. Tomorrow, repeat steps 2–4

6. Keep going

Which of these options are reasonable and doable, given your unique life?

Option A: Repeat each day (i.e. seven days per week), keeping an unbroken chain of progress for as long as you can.

Option B: Select a day off per week, so that you're spending at least an hour a day on your top project six times during the week.

Option C: Aim to do your Magic Hour at least five days a week.

Option D: Aim to do your Magic Hour at least four days a week.

Option E: Aim to do your Magic Hour at least three days a week.

Note: I'm a big advocate of taking an hour a day because it's enough time to make substantial progress that accrues quick benefits. HOWEVER, it could be that you can't swing sixty minutes, given your life situation. **Do what makes sense for you.** Try thirty minutes a day instead. Or fifteen minutes a day. Or ten minutes. Or even five. The actual amount of time per day doesn't really matter. *If you keep at it, you will make progress.* If you put in five minutes a day consistently, you will get there eventually. It will take longer than if you had sixty minutes a day to devote to the task but you *will* arrive at the same destination.

CHAPTER 9

Using Life Levers to Improve Your Life

© Lisa Rothstein, www.LisaRothstein.com

As we have seen in the previous chapters, Life Levers are helpful for solving specific problems and for accomplishing particular goals. Interestingly, Life Levers can improve things in your life even when you don't really know what you want. Maybe you just feel "off" or "blah" or unfulfilled. Perhaps you have a vague sense that you are missing out. Try applying the Life Lever Approach.

Just make one tiny shift in thought, word, feeling, or deed and watch what happens. If you sense positive results, carry on. Monitor and adjust accordingly. If things seem unchanged, try a different Lever.

If you have no idea which Lever to use, you could try one of the three highly effective Levers examined in earlier chapters—Gratitude, Forgiveness, or Mindfulness. These are simple Levers that work wonders.

Alternatively, you could use the activities in this chapter to identify a Lever unique to your current life, circumstances, and preferences.

PREPARATION STEP: EXAMINE YOUR CURRENT SITUATION

Clear some uninterrupted time for some candid personal reflection.

1. How do you feel about your current life? What emotions do you experience on most days?

TROUBLESHOOTING

If you need more prompts, complete the following sentence fragments:

I'm sad that...

I'm disappointed...

I'm resentful...

I'm mad because...

I'm upset...

I'm worried...

I'm embarrassed...

I regret...

I'm hurt...

I'm afraid...

I don't like...

I'm frustrated that...

I'm annoyed by...

I hate...

I like...

I love...

I feel...

2. What do you think about your current life? What are your recurring thoughts these days? *(Option: Carry this book around with you for the next few days, as thoughts occur to you, capture them here.)*

TROUBLESHOOTING

If you need more prompts, complete the following sentence fragments:

It seems...

I see that...

I understand...

I believe...

I know...

I wonder...

I don't know...

I need...

I want...

I don't want...

3. Describe your current life.

4. Re-read your response to question #3. What do you notice about the words you use to describe your current situation? What patterns do you see? Any surprises?

5. Go back through each response to questions #1–3. Is it accurate? Are there things you are exaggerating or downplaying? For each item, ask yourself:
    - Is this actually true?
    - Is there evidence that proves it?
    - If not, what is true?
    - What are the facts here?

Revise your answers to reflect what is actually true.
    - Cross out what is untrue.
    - Change words to more accurately reflect your current situation.

6. Once you have re-written your answers to be accurate and truthful, consider any discrepancies between the objective situation and how you have been describing your current life. Going forward, what change in words or framing could you make that might improve the situation? Be specific. Revise accordingly.

7. Next, ask: How are my actions contributing to my current view of my life?

TROUBLESHOOTING

If you need more prompts, complete the following sentence fragments:

I've been...

I'm doing...

I'm trying...

I'm...

I'm not...

I'm avoiding...

The purpose of the preceding Preparation Step is to generate ideas and insights so you can apply the Life Lever Approach.

STEP ONE: CHOOSE A TINY CHANGE AS YOUR LEVER

As you think about your current life, what tiny change in thought, word, feelings, or deed might improve your life?

Pick something—anything—as your Lever.

STEP TWO: START

Begin.

TROUBLESHOOTING

If you find yourself hesitating to get started, refer to the troubleshooting techniques listed for Step Two in Chapter 3.

STEP THREE: CARRY ON. MONITOR AND ADJUST ACCORDINGLY

MONITOR YOUR PROGRESS

A. Keep Track

- What are simple, easy ways you can track your progress?

B. Analyze

Schedule an appointment with yourself for a month from now. On that date, pause to answer the following:

- Overall, how are you doing, compared with how you were when you started? How do you feel about your life?

- What changes have you noticed?

- What's working well?

- What's not?

- Going forward, what adjustments are needed, if any?

C. Adjust accordingly

If you are experiencing improvements in your life, carry on.

If adjustments are needed, do what makes sense. When it seems like you should do more or less, do so. if it's time to switch Levers, do so.

CHAPTER 10

What Works Best for You?

As you experiment with different Life Levers, it's helpful to recognize and make note of your most effective tools. Actually make a list of what works well for you. Put it somewhere you will see regularly—in your phone, on your computer, or inside your toothbrush cabinet.

First, this is a way of keeping you on track.

Second, should you have a new goal to achieve or a new problem to solve or if you find yourself feeling "off", you have a list of immediate remedies you can apply.

It may not be complicated or fancy, but this simple technique works. It's an easy, effective way to combat our natural internal resistance. Somehow, left to our own devices, we humans tend to "forget" or stop doing things that work well for us.

For example, if you've had the experience of losing weight, you've figured out what works for you. What often happens, however, is that when you reach your goal weight and conclude dieting, it doesn't take long before you slide back into old habits. Before you know it, the pounds can creep back.

Now imagine, instead, that at the conclusion of your diet, you took a few moments to write down what you've found works for you. For example, when Maria got to her goal weight, she wrote the following:

I will weigh myself every day and record my weight.
If my weight is two pounds heavier than my preferred base

weight, I will reduce my food intake until I'm within a pound of my target weight.

I will read the nutritional information on packages so I make good choices when food shopping.

I will avoid buying junk food so it's not in the house tempting me.

I will drink a glass of water before every meal. I will eat at least one salad per day.

I will avoid eating after 7 pm at night.

When I eat in a restaurant, I will be aware of the portion sizes and take action accordingly. If the serving is too large, I won't feel compelled to eat everything. It's okay to leave food on my plate or to take home leftovers for subsequent meals.

By writing out what works for you, you have a handy reminder. You can keep yourself at your preferred weight more easily and purposefully.

And if at some point in the future, your clothing feels snug, you can refer to your list. Of these items, what are you doing? What have you let slip? What adjustments can you make, going forward?

You can apply the same approach to make the most of your experiences trying different Life Levers. Add them to the "What Works for Me" list on the following page. Going forward, as you find new, helpful approaches or Levers, add them to your list.

Whenever you have a problem to solve or a task to accomplish or a desire to shift things in your life, refer to your list.

WHAT WORKS FOR ME

What helps me solve problems?

What helps me get things done?

What helps me enjoy my life more?

What practices have I found helpful?

What tiny shifts in thought have worked well for me?

What tiny shifts in behavior have worked well for me?

What tiny shifts in feeling have worked well for me?

What tiny shifts in words have worked well for me?

Acknowledgements

Special thanks to *New Yorker* cartoonist Lisa Rothstein for the cartoon illustrations throughout this book (www.LisaRothstein.com).

Sincere thanks to Janna Stewart and Paula Gill for reading earlier drafts of this book. Your feedback and suggestions for improvement are most appreciated.

In gratitude for many blessings, a portion of the proceeds of this book is being donated to charity.